Understanding Islam and Christianity made easy

Mark Water

HENDRICKSON
PUBLISHERS

Understanding Islam and Christianity made easy
Hendrickson Publishers, Inc.
P.O. Box 3473
Peabody, Massachusetts 01961-3473

Copyright © 2005 John Hunt Publishing Ltd
Text copyright: © 2005 Mark Water

ISBN 1-56563-582-5

Original text published in English under the title
"Understanding Islam and Christianity made easy"
By John Hunt Publishing Ltd, Deershot Lodge,
Park Lane, Ropley, Hants, SO24 OBE, UK.

Designed by Andrew Milne Design,
www.milnedesign.co.uk

First printing November 2004
Printed by South China Printing Co.,
Hong Kong/China

CONTENTS

500

7-page pull-out chart
7 ways to witness to Muslims

3/07

HOW MANY MUSLIMS ARE THERE?

One billion+

Muslims claim that there are over one billion people who follow the Islamic faith.

About 21% of the world's population is Muslim. So two out of every ten people in the world have embraced Islam.

Christianity and Islam

At the moment Christianity is the world's largest major religion. But its rate of increase has not been keeping up with the phenomenal rate of increase of Islam.

About 33% of the world's population are Christians, at least in name. This has been the proportion for a number of decades. But this position is about to change dramatically. In a decade or two, if present trends continue, there will be more Muslims in the world than Christians.

Fastest growing faith

Out of the all the major world faiths the Islamic faith is the fastest growing global religion.

AREAS OF THE WORLD MOST POPULATED BY MUSLIMS	
Area of world	*Percentage of all Muslims*
Indian subcontinent	30%
Sub-Saharan Africa	20%
Arab world	18%
Southeast Asia	17%
Soviet Union and China	10%

"Muslims are the world's fastest-growing group," according to *The Population Reference Bureau*.

Influence of Islam

Adherents to the Islamic faith do not just subscribe to a religion. They follow a carefully defined way of life.

Where do Muslims live?

It is wrong to think that most Muslims are Arabs. However, about 18% of the world's Muslims do live in the Arab world.

The three non-Arab Middle Eastern countries with the most Muslims are Turkey, Iran, and Afghanistan.

Muslims in America

"Islam is the fastest-growing religion in America, a guide and pillar of stability for many of our people," wrote Hillary Clinton, in the *Los Angeles Times*.

There are about five million Muslims in the United States.

MUSLIM SECTS AND MUSLIM GOVERNMENTS

1 Sects

Like other major world faiths Islam has numerous divisions or sects within it.

SECT	LOCATION	CHARACTERISTICS
SUNNI (The Sunni Muslims are the dominant form of Islam.)	Spread throughout the world in: Egypt, Yemen, Oman, Jordan, Palestine, United Arab Emirates (UAE), Turkey, Bangladesh, Pakistan, Indonesia, and Malaysia.	Sunni Muslims are usually the most tolerant and peaceful of the Muslims. They usually have secular governments.
SHIA	Shia Muslims are strongest in: Syria, Iraq, Iran, and Pakistan.	Shia Muslims have the reputation for being more militant and radical than the Sunni Muslims.
SUFI	Sufi Muslims live in Pakistan and Iran.	Renowned for their emphasis on meditation and often enter into trance-like states. They concentrate on the mystical side of Islam.
WAHHABI	Saudi Arabia.	They are a very a conservative sect, and interpret Islamic law very rigidly. They are known for their honesty, but appear to be intolerant toward those who break their laws.

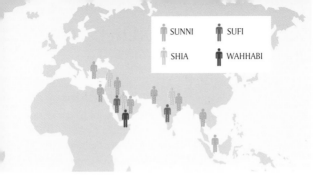

SUNNI	SUFI	SHIA	WAHHABI

2 Governments

SECULAR GOVERNMENTS

Islamic countries are governed in a variety of ways.

Secular Islamic countries, including Indonesia, Syria, Bangladesh, Pakistan, Egypt, Libya, Turkey, Iraq, Tunisia, Algeria, and Mali, are governed by Muslim leaders who do not impose their religion on the country. They do not allow *Sharia* law to be strictly enforced. They are reasonably tolerant toward non-Muslims.

ISLAMIC KINGDOMS

The Islamic kingdoms and sheikdoms of Saudi Arabia, Oman, UAE, Kuwait, Yemen, and Morocco have rulers who take the Muslim religion very seriously indeed. They do not allow Christians to evangelize in their countries.

MINORITY ISLAM COUNTRIES

An increasing number of countries have a large and growing Muslim population.

COUNTRY	ESTIMATED MUSLIM POPULATION
India	More than 100 million
China	20 to 50 million
France	5 million Muslims
USA	5 million
Britain	1-2 million

These countries are finding that Muslims are beginning to flex their political muscles more and more.

THE FIVE PILLARS OF ISLAM

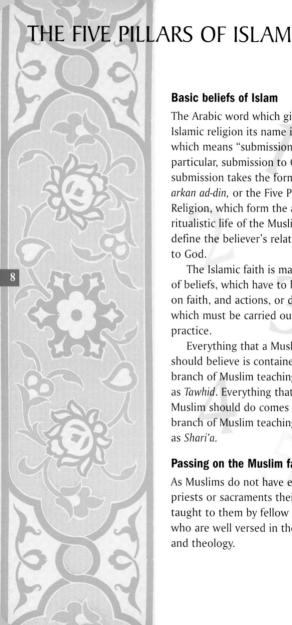

Basic beliefs of Islam

The Arabic word which gives Islamic religion its name is *islam,* which means "submission," in particular, submission to God. This submission takes the form of the *arkan ad-din,* or the Five Pillars of Religion, which form the active ritualistic life of the Muslim and define the believer's relationship to God.

The Islamic faith is made up of beliefs, which have to be taken on faith, and actions, or duty *(din),* which must be carried out in practice.

Everything that a Muslim should believe is contained in the branch of Muslim teaching known as *Tawhid*. Everything that a Muslim should do comes in the branch of Muslim teaching known as *Shari'a.*

Passing on the Muslim faith

As Muslims do not have either priests or sacraments their faith is taught to them by fellow Muslims who are well versed in their law and theology.

The five Pillars

The basics of Muslim faith and practice are found in their five Pillars of Islam.

Every Muslim is expected to perform the duties contained in these five Pillars:

1 FAITH

2 PRAYER

3 TITHE

4 THE FAST

5 THE PILGRIMAGE

The Prophet Muhammad was reported to have said, "Islam is based upon five pillars: to make *Shahada* (declaration of faith), to establish *Salat* (formal prayer), to give *Zakat* (charity), to make *Sawm* (fasting in the month of Ramadan), to perform *Hajj* (pilgrimage to the Ka'bah)."

THE FIVE PILLARS OF ISLAM: 1 FAITH (the Shahada)

Faith *(the Shahada)*

This is the most important of the five Pillars of the Muslim faith.

It is their creed *(Kalima)*, or summary of their basic religious belief.

Shahada

This declaration of faith is called the *Shahada*. It is short and simple.

"There is no God but Allah, and Muhammad is the Prophet of Allah."

Muslims say this when they wake up in the morning, and just before they go to sleep at night.

Details of the *Shahada*

From this testimony of faith it is clear that Muslims are monotheistic, as they believe in only one God.

A transliteration of the *Shahada* is as follows: "La ilaha illa Allah, Muhammadur rasoolu Allah."

The first part, "La ilaha illa Allah" means that, "There is no true god (deity) but God (Allah)."

The last part, "Muhammadur rasoolu Allah," means that Muhammad is God's Messenger (Prophet). God's guidance has come to us through a human being.

A Christian response

GOD NOT ALLAH

Christians believe that they are justified before God, not before Allah. This only comes about through the work of Jesus.

"For it is by grace you have been saved, through faith – and this not from yourselves, it is the gift of God – not by works, so that no one can boast. For we are God's workmanship, created in Christ Jesus to do good works, which God prepared in advance for us to do." *Ephesians 2:8-10*

JESUS NOT MUHAMMAD

"Let us fix our eyes on Jesus, the author and perfecter of our faith." *Hebrews 12:2*

A CHRISTIAN CREDO

Christians declare their faith in verses similar to Romans 6:23, "For the wages of sin is death; but the gift of God is eternal life in Jesus Christ our Lord."

THE FIVE PILLARS OF ISLAM: 2 PRAYER (SALAT)

Five times a day

Prayer, *Salat,* must be observed five times a day by Muslims:

- upon rising
- at noon
- in mid-afternoon
- after sunset
- before going to sleep

The call to prayer

This prayer ritual is central to the life of a devout Muslim. A Muslim crier, the *muezzin,* issues the following call to prayer from a tower, *minaret,* of a mosque.

> "God is most great.
> God is most great.
> God is most great.
> God is most great.
> I testify that there is no god except God.
> I testify that there is no god except God.
> I testify that Muhammad is the messenger of God.
> I testify that Muhammad is the messenger of God.
> Come to prayer!
> Come to prayer!
> Come to success (in this life and the hereafter)!
> Come to success!
> God is most great.
> God is most great.
> There is no god except God."

Ritual

Muslims always pray toward Mecca.

For each segment of the prayer, a Muslim adopts a distinguishing bodily position, beginning with standing and placing hands across the heart, and then bowing and kneeling.

This commitment to prayer as a central part of daily life is something Christians could learn from.

A Christian response

JESUS AND *RITUALISTIC* PRAYER

Jesus spoke against making prayer into a public spectacle. He emphasized the importance of private prayer.

"And when you pray, do not be like the hypocrites, for they love to pray standing in the synagogues and on the street corners to be seen by men. I tell you the truth, they have received their reward in full. But when you pray, go into your room, close the door and pray to your Father, who is unseen. Then your Father, who sees what is done in secret, will reward you. And when you pray, do not keep on babbling like pagans, for they think they will be heard because of their many words. Do not be like them, for your Father knows what you need before you ask him." *Matthew 6:5-8*

THE FIVE PILLARS OF ISLAM: 3
TITHE (Zakat)

Almsgiving

Almsgiving, *Zakat*, is the third of the five pillars. It is believed that it helps one achieve salvation.

How much?

According to Muhammad: "Charity is a necessity for every Muslim."

Muslims have to give at least one-fortieth, that is 2.5%, of their income to the poor. This practice is said to date back to Muhammad's experience when he was an orphan and longed to help those who had nothing.

Zakat

Zakat means two things: "purification" and "growth." By giving away a proportion of one's possessions to the needy the possessions themselves are thought to be purified. As possessions are cut back in this way they will encourage new growth, like a plant that is pruned.

Zakat is not a voluntary act but a requirement for Muslims.

Sadaqa

In addition to giving away 2.5% of their capital Muslims may also give as much as they like as sadaqa. Sadaqa can be translated as "voluntary charity." But it embraces the wider idea. Muhammad said: "Even meeting your brother with a cheerful face is charity."

A Christian response

Christians also believe that it is right to give to the poor and that it should be done to the glory of God. But any good deeds should be done as a result of our salvation, as no amount of good deeds can help us attain our salvation.

"For we are God's workmanship, created in Christ Jesus to do good works, which God prepared in advance for us to do." *Ephesians 2:10*

Christians do not believe that the Bible lays down any exact percentage of money that should be given away, such as 2.5%, although many believe that the Old Testament rule of giving away 10% of one's income is a good guideline.

THE FIVE PILLARS OF ISLAM: 4
THE FAST (Sawm)

Benefits

The benefits of this fast are said to be:

- self-control
- self-purification
- devotion to God
- identity with the needy

The moon

Allah was originally a moon god worshiped in Mecca. This influenced Muslims to base their calendar on the moon, rather than on the sun. The fast, *Sawn,* is held annually in the month of Ramadan. As the Muslim calendar is lunar, not solar, Ramadan sometimes falls in summer, and sometimes in winter.

From dawn to dusk

Before sunrise and after sunset Muslims are allowed to live a normal life. But from dawn to dusk, during the month of Ramadan, Muslims abstain from:

- food
- drink
- sexual relations

Exceptions

There are some exceptions to the rules imposed on Muslims during the fast of Ramadan. The sick, elderly, and pregnant, and those who are traveling, are permitted to break the fast. However, later in the year, they must fast again and make up an equal number of days they missed during Ramadan.

If this is not possible, they have to feed a hungry person for every day of the fast they have missed.

The fast does not have to be observed by children and starts for children when they reach puberty.

A Christian response

Christians are not against fasting as such. Indeed Jesus encouraged his followers to fast.

"But the time will come when the bridegroom will be taken from them, and on that day they will fast." *Mark 2:20*

Fasting was never meant to be a spectacle but a time for humbly serving others.

"When you fast, do not look somber as the hypocrites do, for they disfigure their faces to show men they are fasting. I tell you the truth, they have received their reward in full. But when you fast, put oil on your head and wash your face, so that it will not be obvious to men that you are fasting, but only to your Father, who is unseen; and your Father, who sees what is done in secret, will reward you." *Matthew 6:16-18*

THE FIVE PILLARS OF ISLAM: 5
THE PILGRIMAGE (Hajj) (1)

Hajj

The fifth Pillar of Islam is the Pilgrimage, *Hajj*.

If at all possible Muslims are expected to make a special pilgrimage to Mecca, Hajj, at least once in their lifetime.

Like the other four pillars of Islam the *Hajj* is essential if one is to gain salvation. So if one is too poor or ill ever to travel to Mecca oneself, someone else is sent to go on the pilgrimage in one's place.

The rituals of *Hajj*

There are a number of rituals and ceremonies in the *Hajj*.

Clothes

Male pilgrims wear a distinctive attire of simple garments to strip away distinctions of class and culture, so that all stand equal before God.

The *Ka'ba*

The whole of the pilgrimage centers on the *Ka'ba*. It is the most sacred building of Islam and is located in the center of the Holy Mosque in Mecca.

The *Ka'ba* consists of a tall, rectangular, box-like structure 45 feet high with sides measuring 32 feet by 36 feet.

The Black Stone, which may have been a meteorite originally, is built into the eastern corner of the structure. Also at the western

corner is another stone known as *Hajar as'ad,* the Lucky Stone, or the Stone of Good Fortune, which is touched while the Pilgrims encircle the *Ka'ba.*

This giant square house is covered with a black cloth and lies in the center of a large square court. It is encircled seven times by the pilgrims.

Muslims, facing Mecca when they pray, are in particular facing the Ka'ba, which they believe was built by Abraham and Ishmael.

They believe that God commanded Abraham to call everyone to visit this place. Today, as pilgrims go there they say, "At Thy service, O Lord," as a response to Abraham's summons.

Pilgrims also go seven times between the mountains of Safa and Marwa, copying Hagar's search for water. Then the pilgrims assemble on the plain of Arafa and pray for God's forgiveness.

Stones are also thrown at a hill outside the court to symbolize the driving away of evil spirits.

THE FIVE PILLARS OF ISLAM: THE PILGRIMAGE (Hajj) (2)

The *Eid al-Adha*

The *Hajj* ends with a festival called the *Eid al-Adha*. An animal such as a sheep or goat is sacrificed to commemorate Abraham's willingness to sacrifice his son for God.

This important Muslim festival also consists of a celebration of prayers and the giving and receiving of gifts by Muslims wherever they are.

The *Eid al-Adha* and the feast day commemorating the end of Ramadan are the two main festivals of the Muslim calendar.

A Christian response

The Muslim pilgrimage focuses on the black stone in the *Ka'ba*, which is its most sacred shrine. But it is not a shrine at all as far as Christians are concerned.

GOD IS NOT IN ANY ONE EARTHLY LOCATION

God is everywhere, and he can be worshiped anywhere.

> "This is what the LORD says:
> 'Heaven is my throne,
> and the earth is my footstool.
> Where is the house you will build for me?
> Where will my resting place be?
> Has not my hand made all these things,
> and so they came into being?'
> declares the LORD.
> 'This is the one I esteem:
> he who is humble and contrite in spirit,
> and trembles at my word.'" *Isaiah 66:1-2*

WHERE SHOULD WE WORSHIP?

Answering a question about where we should worship, Jesus once said:

> "Believe me, woman, a time is coming when you will worship the Father neither on this mountain nor in Jerusalem. You Samaritans worship what you do not know; we worship what we do know, for salvation is from the Jews. Yet a time is coming and has now come when the true worshipers will worship the Father in spirit and truth, for they are the kind of worshipers the Father seeks." *John 4:21-23*

THE FIVE ARTICLES OF FAITH: 1 GOD (1)

Main Islamic teaching

The Five Articles of Faith are the main doctrines of Islam.
Just as all Muslims are required to perform all the Five Pillars of
Islam, so all Muslims are expected to believe in the Five Articles
of Faith.

The Five Articles

The Five Articles are about the following five topics:

- God
- Angles
- Scripture
- Prophets
- The last days

"The Messenger believes in what was sent down to him from his Lord, and the believers; each one believes in God and his angels, and in His Books and His Messengers." *Quran 2:285*

God

For Muslims, "There is only one true God and his name is Allah."

Allah is:

- One

  Muslims have a strong belief in the oneness of God.

- Unique
- Incomparable
- All-knowing
- All-powerful
- The sovereign judge

Not a personal God

Allah is so far removed and greater than humans that he is not thought of as a being a personal God. It is not possible to personally know Allah.

Allah

Muslims believe that they initially become Muslims by sincerely saying: "There is one God – Allah, and his Prophet is Muhammad."

Only Allah should be worshiped. In the Quran, God describes himself as follows:

"Say, 'He is God, the One. God, to whom the creatures turn for their needs. He begets not, nor was He begotten, and there is none like Him." *Quran 112:1-4*

THE FIVE ARTICLES OF FAITH: 1 GOD (2)

A Christian response

Christians do not believe that the Allah of Islam is the same as the God and Father of our Lord Jesus Christ.

ALLAH

Christians do not believe that God can only be referred to as Allah. In the Bible, God is referred to many ways.

"I appeared to Abraham, to Isaac and to Jacob as God Almighty." *Exodus 6:3*

GOD IS PERSONAL

Christians believe that God, as well as being the mighty Creator, and being all-knowing and all-powerful, is a personal God whom we can have a relationship with.

This is demonstrated by:

- **Jesus becoming a human being**

  "The Word became flesh and made his dwelling among us. We have seen his glory, the glory of the One and Only, who came from the Father, full of grace and truth." *John 1:14*

- **Jesus dying for us**

  " . . . I lay down my life for the sheep." *John 10:15*

- **Jesus sending us the Holy Spirit**

  "But when he, the Spirit of truth, comes, he will guide you into all truth. He will not speak on his own; he will speak only what he hears, and he will tell you what is yet to come. He will bring glory to me by taking from what is mine and making it known to you." *John 16:13-14*

LOVE

Christians have solid grounds for believing that God is love.

"This is how God showed his love among us: He sent his one and only Son into the world that we might live through him. If anyone acknowledges that Jesus is the Son of God, God lives in him and he in God. And so we know and rely on the love God has for us. God is love. Whoever lives in love lives in God, and God in him." *1 John 4:9,15-16*

ONE SHEEP

Jesus pictures God the Father as a shepherd who goes out of his way to find and recover one straying sheep.

"What do you think? If a man owns a hundred sheep, and one of them wanders away, will he not leave the ninety-nine on the hills and go to look for the one that wandered off? And if he finds it, I tell you the truth, he is happier about that one sheep than about the ninety-nine that did not wander off. In the same way your Father in heaven is not willing that any of these little ones should be lost." *Matthew 18:12-14*

THE FIVE ARTICLES OF FAITH: 2 ANGELS

Angels

Muslims believe that angels are good spiritual beings. They also believe in *djinns,* evil spiritual beings.

The angels worship God and obey his every command.

Gabriel

Muslims believe that Allah's messages were sent to Muhammad by the agency of the angel Gabriel. He is said to have given the revelations in the Quran to Muhammad.

A Christian response

GABRIEL

The Bible mentions the angel Gabriel in Daniel 8:16: "And I heard a man's voice from the Ulai calling, 'Gabriel, tell this man the meaning of the vision.'"

In the New Testament Gabriel speaks to Zechariah:

"The angel answered, 'I am Gabriel. I stand in the presence of God, and I have been sent to speak to you and to tell you this good news.'" *Luke 1:19*

GABRIEL AND MUHAMMAD

Christians do not believe that Gabriel appeared to Muhammad, if for no other reason than that no obedient angel could have been party to teaching a different gospel than the true one given by Jesus.

"But even if we or an angel from heaven should preach a gospel other than the one we preached to you, let him be eternally condemned!" *Galatians 1:8*

THE FIVE ARTICLES OF FAITH: 3 SCRIPTURE

Quran

What the Old Testament is to Jews, and what the whole Bible is to Christians, the Quran is to Muslims.

Muslims believe that God has ensured that the Quran is free of any corruption or distortion.

A Christian response

Christians believe that no other book supercedes the Bible. Christians do not believe that the Bible is in error or has been corrupted.

Christians believe that nothing should be added to or taken away from the Bible.

"I warn everyone who hears the words of the prophecy of this book: If anyone adds anything to them, God will add to him the plagues described in this book. And if anyone takes words away from this book of prophecy, God will take away from him his share in the tree of life and in the holy city, which are described in this book."
Revelation 22:18-19

THE FIVE ARTICLES OF FAITH: 4 PROPHETS

Prophets and messengers of God

Muslims, in the fourth of their Five Articles of Faith, accept the belief in prophets and messengers of God. They believe that five of the six greatest prophets are among the people mentioned in the Bible.

- Ada (1)
- Noah (2)
- Abraham (3)
- Moses (4)
- Jesus (5)

(1)

(2) (3)

Muhammad *the* prophet

Muslims believe that God's last word to humankind came through his prophet and messenger Muhammad. So Muhammad was the last prophet God sent.

"Muhammad is not the father of any one of your men, but

(4)

(5)

A Christian response

Christians believe that Adam, Noah, Abraham, Moses, and Jesus were prophets. But there is no prophecy in the Bible about Muhammad. Christians do not accept that he was a prophet sent by God, or one through whom God spoke.

DID MOSES PROPHECY ABOUT MUHAMMAD?
See pages 54-55.

he is the Messenger of God and the last of the prophets."
Quran 33:40

Muslims believe that all the prophets and messengers were created human beings who had none of the divine qualities of God.

THE FIVE ARTICLES OF FAITH: 5 THE LAST DAYS

The Day of Judgment

The fifth particular doctrine Muslims are required to believe concerns the last days, another name for the Day of Judgment.

Last days

On the last day there will be a time of resurrection and judgment. Those who follow Allah and Muhammad will go to Islamic heaven, or Paradise. On that day Muslims believe that everyone will be resurrected for God's judgment according to their beliefs and deeds. Those who have not followed Allah will go to hell.

Paradise

Muslims promise their followers entrance to heaven through the door to eternal paradise.

"And give good news (O Muhammad) to those who believe and do good deeds, that they will have gardens (Paradise) in which rivers flow."
Quran 2:25

"God has also said: Race one with another for forgiveness from your Lord and for Paradise, whose width is as the width of the heavens and the earth, which has been prepared for those who believe in God and His messengers." *Quran 57:21*

Muslims believe that if you enter Paradise, you will live a very happy life without sickness, pain, sadness, or death; God will be pleased with you; and you will live there forever.

A rather sensuous heaven

Islamic heaven is pictured as a place where the faithful will enjoy many lustful pleasures, including sexual relations with virgins, and exotic food and drink.

"They shall recline on jeweled couches face to face, and there shall wait on them immortal youths with bowls and ewers and a cup of purest wine, with fruits of their own choice and flesh of fowls that they relish. And theirs shall be the celestial virgins, chaste as hidden pearls: a reward for their deeds." *Quran 56:15*

A Christian response

For Christians, heaven is not contaminated by earthly and sensuous desires. The kingdom of God is not a matter of eating and drinking. See Romans 14:17.

In heaven Christians will not even be married, but will be like angels. See Matthew 22:30.

In heaven Christians will have resurrected bodies, and pain and tears will be no more. "He will wipe every tear from their eyes. There will be no more death or mourning or crying or pain, for the old order of things has passed away." *Revelation 21:4*

OTHER ISLAMIC BELIEFS: SALVATION

Only through Allah

According to Muslim teaching, salvation comes only through Allah. Only those who obey Allah and Muhammad his prophet can enter heaven.

"If anyone desires a religion other than Islam (submission to Allah), Never will it be accepted of him; and in the Hereafter he will be in the ranks of those who have lost." *Quran 3:85*

"He has prepared, for those who reject Allah, a Blazing Fire!" *Quran 48:13*

Happiness and peace

The Islamic faith says that it offers real happiness and inner peace if we submit to the commands of the Creator and the Sustainer of this world. For God has said in the Quran:

"Truly, in remembering God do hearts find rest." *Quran 13:28*

A life of hardship awaits those who reject the teaching of the Quran.

"God has said: But whoever turns away from the Quran, he will have a hard life, and We will raise him up blind on the Day of Judgment." *Quran 20:124*

Cat Stevens

Muslims point to their high-profile converts to underline the truth of their religion. Cat Stevens, who now goes by the name of Yusuf Islam, earned more than $150,000 a night as a world-famous pop star.

However, after he converted to Islam, he testifies that he found true happiness and peace, which he had not found in all his previous material success.

Forgiveness of sins

God forgives all of the previous sins of converts to Islam.

Muslims recount the story about a man called Amr who came to the Prophet Muhammad and said, "Give me your right hand so that I may give you my pledge of loyalty."

The Prophet stretched out his right hand but Amr withdrew his hand. So the Prophet said: "What has happened to you, O Amr?"

He replied, "I intend to lay down a condition."

The Prophet asked: "What condition do you intend to put forward?"

Amr said, "That God forgive my sins."

The Prophet said: "Didn't you know that converting to Islam erases all previous sins?

A Christian response

Christians insist that salvation comes only through Jesus Christ.

"Salvation is found in no one else, for there is no other name under heaven given to men by which we must be saved." *Acts 4:12*

See also: John 8:24; 10:1-2,9; 14:6; Revelation 5:1-9; 1 John 2:22-23; Isaiah 43:11; Hosea 13:4; 1 Timothy 2:5

OTHER ISLAMIC BELIEFS: PREDESTINATION

It is the will of Allah

Muslims believe in divine predestination, *Al-Qadar*. But they also believe that humans have free will. So humans are able to choose between good and evil and are responsible for their choices.

Al-Qadar

This belief in divine predestination includes belief that:

- God knowing everything
- God has recorded all that has happened and all that will happen
- Whatever happens is according to God's wills
- God is the Creator of everything.

Quran and divine providence

". . . so whoever is willing, he may take a path to his Lord. And you do not will unless God wills." *Quran 76:29-30*

"Thou makest to err . . . whomever Thou pleasest and guidest whomever Thou pleasest." *Quran 7:155*

A Christian response

Christians do not believe in a fatalistic approach to life. They believe that the Bible teaches both divine predestination and human responsibility.

"Whoever is thirsty, let him come; and whoever wishes, let him take the free gift of the water of life." *Revelation 22:17*

". . . that everyone who believes in him may have eternal life. For God so loved the world that he gave his one and only Son, that whoever believes in him shall not perish but have eternal life." *John 3:15-16*

OTHER ISLAMIC BELIEFS: ORIGINAL SIN

Islam's rejection of original sin

Muslims do not believe in original sin. Rather, they believe that all children are born with an innate disposition towards virtue, knowledge, and beauty, *fitra*.

They believe that they must live in this life in such a way that they return to their original good nature.

Muhammad and sin

Muhammad said, "Every human being is born in a state of a pure nature; but through the influence of his parents, he may become non-Muslim."

Muslims and sin

For a Muslim, sin is not obeying Allah. They believe that we do commit sinful actions, but not that we are sinful by nature.

Muslims do not view Jesus as their own Savior from sin. They do not believe that they are innately sinful and in need of a savior at all in this sense.

A Christian response

The Bible teaches that we were born into sin, Genesis 3, and that spiritual death spread to all humankind. See Psalm 51:5; Romans 5:12,14.

Christians believe that everyone is sinful by nature.

". . . for all have sinned and fall short of the glory of God." *Romans 3:23*

"All of us also lived among them at one time, gratifying the cravings of our sinful nature and following its desires and thoughts. Like the rest, we were by nature objects of wrath." *Ephesians 2:3*

"If we claim we have not sinned, we make him out to be a liar and his word has no place in our lives." *1 John 1:10*

See also: 2 Chronicles 6:36; Isaiah 53:6; Romans 3:10,12,23; 5:12,14; 11:32.

COMPARING DOCTRINAL BELIEFS (1)

	THE AFTERLIFE	ANGELS
MUSLIM	There is an afterlife, Quran 75:12. This will be experienced in Paradise, Quran 29:64, by faithful Muslims, but in hell for those who do not embrace the Muslim faith.	Muslims believe that angels are created beings who serve God.
CHRISTIAN	Christians will live in heaven with their Lord, Philippians 1:21-24, where they will have resurrected bodies, 1 Corinthians 15:50-58. Non-Christians will be in hell, Matthew 25:46.	 Christians also believe that angels are created beings who serve God.

Major differences

Islam and Christianity do not just have a few differences over unimportant details when it comes to their respective beliefs. They have major differences.

ATONEMENT	THE BIBLE
While Muslims do confess sin and believe in repentance they do not believe in the need for any atonement for sin. They do not believe that they have a sinful nature that needs radical attention.	For Muslims the Bible is respected for being the word of the prophets. However, they believe that the Bible has been corrupted through the centuries and is only correct in so far as it agrees with the Quran.
Central to Christian belief is the sacrifice of Jesus on the cross. "He is the atoning sacrifice for our sins, and not only for ours but also for the sins of the whole world." *1 John 2:2* This sacrifice needs to be embraced and accepted by each human being, John 1:12. This is done by faith: "Therefore, since we have been justified through faith, we have peace with God through our Lord Jesus Christ." *Romans 5:1*	For Christians, the Bible is the inspired Word of God and has no errors in the original manuscripts. See 2 Timothy 3:16.

COMPARING DOCTRINAL BELIEFS (2)

	THE CRUCIFIXION OF JESUS	THE DEVIL
MUSLIM	Muslims do not believe that Jesus died on the cross. Rather, that God allowed Judas to look like Jesus and to be crucified instead of Jesus.	Muslims believe that the devil, *Iblis,* is a fallen *jinn,* who was created from fire. He is neither an angel nor a man, but a created being with free will.
CHRISTIAN	Christians emphasize that the crucifixion of Jesus was an historic fact and that Jesus died for the sins of the world. "Christ redeemed us from the curse of the law by becoming a curse for us, for it is written: 'Cursed is everyone who is hung on a tree.'" *Galatians 3:13*	Christians believe that the devil is a fallen angel. He sets about destroying human beings and actively opposes God's will. See Ezekiel 28:13-15; 1 Peter 5:8

GOD	THE QURAN
God, that is, Allah, is one person, and no other God exists. Allah is the creator of the universe, Quran 3:191, and reigns over all, Quran 6:61-62.	For Muslims, the Quran is God's final revelation to humankind. It was mediated through archangel Gabriel to Muhammad over a period of more than twenty years. Allah ensured that it is free of any kind of error.
While Christians do believe that a trinity of persons, the Father, Son, and Holy Spirit make up the Godhead, they do not believe in three gods, but in one God.	Christians do not accept the Quran as being in any way divinely inspired. Rather they attribute it to Muhammad.

SAYINGS OF THE PROPHET MUHAMMAD

Employers

"Pay the worker his wage before his sweat dries."

Mercy

"God has no mercy on one who has no mercy for others."
"The merciful are shown mercy by the All-Merciful. Show mercy to those on earth, and God will show mercy to you."

The poor

"He who eats his fill while his neighbor goes without food is not a believer."

Brotherly love

"None of you truly believes until he wishes for his brother what he wishes for himself."

Charity

"Smiling at your brother is charity."
"A good word is charity."

Anger

"Powerful is not he who knocks the other down, indeed powerful is he who controls himself in a fit of anger."

God sees into your heart

"God does not judge according to your bodies and appearances but He scans your hearts and looks into your deeds."

Like a body

"The believers, in their love, mercy, and kindness to one another are like a body: if any part of it is ill, the whole body shares its sleeplessness and fever."

Wives

"The most perfect of the believers in faith are the best of them in morals. And the best among them are those who are best to their wives."

ISLAMIC LAW

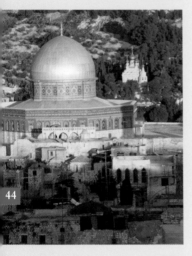

Sharia

Islamic law is called *Sharia*. Its main sources are the Quran and the *Hadith*. *Sharia* contains religious laws which govern the cultural life of Islam. Sharia is followed by Sunni Muslims and Shia Muslims, but not by Sufi Muslims.

Sharia, or Islamic law, is a body of law developed in much the same manner as the Jewish Talmudic law.

Muslims draw no distinctions between religious and secular life, so *Sharia* covers all aspects of religion, government, and every other area of daily life.

Hadith

The *Hadith* are laws, legends, and stories about Muhammad's way of life.

For most Muslims, the *Hadith* contains an authoritative exposition of the meaning of the Quran.

No alcohol, no gambling

Gambling and drunkenness are prohibited.

"O you who believe, intoxicants and games of chance are only an uncleanness, the devil's work; so shun it, that you may succeed. The devil desires only to create enmity and hatred among you by means of intoxicants and games of chance, and to prevent you from the remembrance of God and from prayer. So will you obey this prohibition?" *Quran 5:90-91*

More Muslim laws

- No smoking tobacco
- No eating of pork products
- No pornography
- Women must dress modestly and are under control of their fathers or husbands.
- Non-Muslims may not enter most mosques

Sexual morality

The Quran speaks against fornication and adultery.

"Nor come nigh to adultery: for it is a shameful (deed) and an evil, opening the road (to other evils)." *Quran 17:32*

"Those who invoke not, with Allah, any other god, nor slay such life as Allah has made sacred except for just cause, nor commit fornication . . " *Quran 25:68*

"And go not nigh to fornication; surely it is an obscenity. And evil is the way." *Quran 17:32*

MUSLIMS AND JESUS

Respect

As far as Christians are concerned the acid test of any religion is what it thinks of Jesus.

Muslims do respect Jesus. They think of him as a very important prophet. In fact he is one of the six greatest prophets, along with Adam, Noah, Abraham, Moses, and Muhammad.

Not the Son of God

Muslims deny the deity of Jesus, that Jesus is the Son of God.

"The Messiah, Jesus the son of Mary, was no more than Allah's apostle and His Word which He cast to Mary; a spirit from Him. So believe in Allah and His apostles and do not say: 'Three.' . . . Allah is but one God." *Quran 4:171*

Jesus and the Trinity

Muslims affirm the unity of God. They reject the divinity of Christ and the doctrine of the Trinity.

A Christian response

JESUS WAS MORE THAN A PROPHET

JESUS CLAIMED TO BE GOD

"But he continued, 'You are from below; I am from above. You are of this world; I am not of this world.'" *John 8:23*

"I and the Father are one." *John 10:30*

See also: John 4:26; 13:13; 14:7-10; Matthew 17:5; Mark 1:1; Luke 1:35; Philippians 2:6; Hebrews 1:8; 1 John 4:15.

JESUS ACCEPTED WORSHIP

"Then they worshiped him and returned to Jerusalem with great joy." *Luke 24:52*

"Jesus heard that they had thrown him out, and when he found him, he said, 'Do you believe in the Son of Man?' 'Who is he, sir?' the man asked. 'Tell me so that I may believe in him.' Jesus said, 'You have now seen him; in fact, he is the one speaking with you.' Then the man said, 'Lord, I believe,' and he worshiped him." *John 9:35-38*

See also: Matthew 8:2; 9:18; 14:33; 15:25; 18:26; 28:9,17; Mark 5:6.

JESUS FORGAVE SINS

See Matthew 9:6; Mark 2:7.

JESUS LIVED A SINLESS LIFE

JESUS WAS RAISED FROM THE DEAD

MUHAMMAD AND JESUS

Son of God, or just another "son" of God?

The New Testament describes Jesus as the unique "Son" of God and not just another "son" of God, amongst many, in a metaphorical sense.

Hebrews chapter 1 shows clearly the divinity of Christ

"The Son is the radiance of God's glory and the exact representation of his being, sustaining all things by his powerful word. After he had provided purification for sins, he sat down at the right hand of the Majesty in heaven." *Hebrews 1:3*

Jesus before Pilate

When Jesus was brought before Pilate the Jews said, "We have a law, and according to that law he must die, because he claimed to be the Son of God." *John 19:7*

If Jesus were only speaking metaphorically the Jews would not have brought him to trial on such a charge as blasphemy. See also Acts 10:38; 1 Peter 2:21-24; 1 John 2:1; 3:5).

Contrasting Jesus with Muhammad

JESUS CALLS HIMSELF THE SON OF GOD

"Moreover, the Father judges no one, but has entrusted all judgment to the Son, that all may honor the Son just they honor the Father. He who does not honor the Son does not honor the Father, who sent him." *John 5:22*

JESUS ELABORATES ON HIS UNIQUE SONSHIP

"All things have been committed to me by my Father. No one knows the Son except the Father, and no one knows the Father except the Son and those to whom the Son chooses to reveal him." *Matthew 11:27*

MUHAMMAD

Muhammad himself admitted that he was a mere mortal. "Say: I am only a mortal like you."

He openly stated that he could not help people, let alone forgive their sins.

"And I do not say to you that I have the treasures of Allah and I do not know the unseen, nor do I say that I am an angel." *Quran 11:31*

Jesus' power came from God and, unlike Muhammad, not from his wealth or political influence.

MUHAMMAD'S LIFE (1)

Birth

Muhammad was born in Mecca (Makkah) in AD 570.

Since his father died before his birth, and his mother shortly afterwards, he was raised by his uncle from the respected tribe of Quraysh.

He was never taught to read or write, and remained illiterate all his life.

But, as he grew up, he became known for his truthfulness, generosity, and sincerity. He arbitrated in disputes between people.

A model of simplicity and humility

Muhammad is portrayed as living a model life. He is remembered for being a
- prophet
- teacher
- statesman
- judge

But he is also revered because he did ordinary things, such as:
- milking his goat
- mending his own clothes
- repairing his shoes
- visiting the poor and the sick
- doing heavy manual work to help his neighbors

Deeply religious nature

Muhammad reacted against the materialism that surrounded him. He used to meditate in a cave, the Cave of Hira near the summit of Jabal al-Nur.

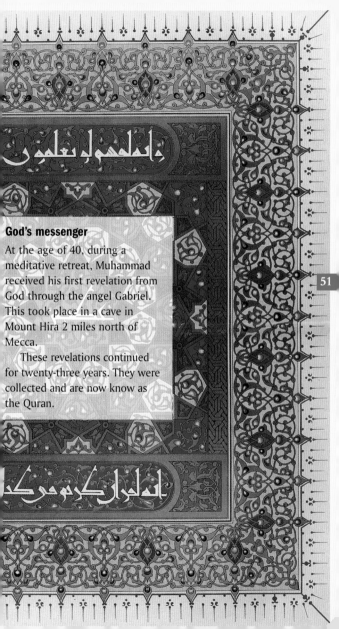

God's messenger

At the age of 40, during a meditative retreat, Muhammad received his first revelation from God through the angel Gabriel. This took place in a cave in Mount Hira 2 miles north of Mecca.

These revelations continued for twenty-three years. They were collected and are now know as the Quran.

MUHAMMAD'S LIFE (2)

Preaching and persecution

As soon as Muhammad began to
recite the words he heard from
Gabriel, and to preach, he and his small
group of followers were persecuted. The group
of people who followed Muhammad's teaching
opposed the idolatry in Mecca and so were very unpopular.
As a result of being persecuted they left Mecca for Medina
some 260 miles to the north. This event, the *Hijra,* is now
known as the "migration."

Medina

In Medina, Muhammad, once a lonely missionary, became
a spiritual and military ruler and conqueror. His religious
teaching shaped the religion of Islam.

In 630 Mecca surrendered to him and he destroyed the idols
in the Ka'ba, a shrine of Arabic pagan gods.

Farewell speech

In 632 Muhammad gave his farewell address from Mount Arafat.
In it he said: "I am leaving you with the Book of God . . . O men
hearken well to my words." He died in 633 in the arms of his
wife Aisha and was buried under her room in Medina.

Muhammad's achievements

Muhammad:
- preached a religion
- founded a state
- built a nation
- laid down a moral code
- initiated numerous social and political reforms
- established a powerful and dynamic society to practice and represent his teachings

Spread of Islam

Before Muhammad died at the age of 63, the greater part of Arabia was Muslim. But when he died he could not have foreseen the future expansion of Islam. Within a century of his death Islam had spread to Spain in the West and as far East as China.

MUHAMMAD'S CLAIMS

Does the Bible prophesy about Muhammad?

Muslims point to biblical prophecies about the coming of the Prophet Muhammad as evidence of the truth of Islam.

In particular they quote from Deuteronomy 18. Moses stated that God told him:

"I will raise up for them a prophet like you from among their brothers; I will put my words in his mouth, and he will tell them everything I command him. If anyone does not listen to my words that the prophet speaks in my name, I myself will call him to account." *Deuteronomy 18:18-19*

A Christian response

The Bible actually tells us who the prophet of Deuteronomy 18:18 is.

[Jesus said:] "If you believed Moses, you would believe me, for he wrote about me." *John 5:46*

PETER QUOTES DEUTERONOMY 18

"The God of Abraham, Isaac and Jacob, the God of our fathers, has glorified his servant Jesus. You handed him over to be killed . . . Now, brothers, I know that you acted in ignorance, as did your leaders. But this is how God fulfilled what he had foretold through all the prophets, saying that his Christ would suffer. Repent, then, and turn to God, so that

Conclusions Muslims Draw from Deuteronomy 18

Muslims conclude from these verses that the prophet in this prophecy must have the following three characteristics:
• he will be like Moses
• he will come from the brothers of the Israelites, i.e. the Ishmaelites
• God will put his words into the mouth of this prophet and that he will speak as God directs him

Muslims insist that the prophet spoken about in Deuteronomy 18:18-19 was Muhammad. Muslims do not claim that Muhammad was divine but the last of the prophets, the one predicted in Moses' day.

your sins may be wiped out, that times of refreshing may come from the Lord, and that he may send the Christ, who has been appointed for you – even Jesus. He must remain in heaven until the time comes for God to restore everything, as he promised long ago through his holy prophets. For Moses said, 'The Lord your God will raise up for you a prophet like me from among your own people; you must listen to everything he tells you. Anyone who does not listen to him will be completely cut off from among his people.'"
Acts 3:13,17-23

These verses indicate that Jesus is the prophet that Moses spoke of.

LOOKING AT THE QURAN

What is the Quran (Koran)?

Muslims believe that the Quran is a record of the exact words revealed by God through the angel Gabriel to the Prophet Muhammad.

"In the month of Ramadan the Quran was revealed, a book of guidance distinguishing right from wrong." *Quran 2:185*

Muhammad, who was illiterate, memorized the words Gabriel told him and then repeated them to his companions. Scribes then recorded these words.

Suras

The Quran consists of one hundred and fourteen chapters, or *suras*.

Accuracy assured

According to the Quran, it is free from any corruption or distortion.

"God has said: Indeed, We have sent down the Quran, and surely We will guard it (from corruption)." *Quran, 15:9*

Every word in the Quran, it is believed, has been miraculously preserved just as it was revealed to Muhammad.

Why is the Quran important?

The Quran is the Scripture of Muslims. It is believed to be the Word of God. It is the prime source of faith and practice for all Muslims.

For the Muslim, the Quran gives them "the right path" (Quran 43:63) to follow.

Topics covered

The Quran's basic theme is the relationship between God and his creatures. It also includes teaching about:
- wisdom
- doctrine
- worship
- law

The Quran and the Bible

Muslims believe that the Bible should be interpreted in the light of the Quran. Christians believe that the Bible, not the Quran, is the genuine Word of God.

"We have revealed the Book with the truth. It confirms the scriptures which came before it and stands as a guardian over them. Therefore give judgment among men according to God's revelations and do not yield to their fancies or swerve from the truth made known to you." *Quran 5:48*

Does the Quran ever contradict the Bible?

The Quran quotes from Psalm 37:29 in Sura 21:105 and agrees with many things stated in the Bible.

However, it claims that the Bible is sometimes inaccurate and wrong in its teaching. Most notably of all the Quran does not agree with the Bible that Jesus was the Son of God, or that Jesus died on the cross.

Damned

Those who reject the Quran are threatened with being damned.

"Those who disbelieve in and reject My communications, they are the inmates of the fire, in it they shall abide." *Quran 2:39*

MUSLIMS AND WOMEN

Women in society

The following verse from the Quran (9:71) shows that both women and men are to take an active role in society rather than merely a passive one.

"And [as for] the believers, both men and women - they are friends and protectors of one another: they [all] enjoin the doing of what is right and forbid the doing of what is wrong, . . . It is they upon whom God will bestow His grace: verily, God is almighty, wise."

Are Muslim women liberated?

Islam views all women, whether single or married, as individuals who have rights, such as owning property and spending her earnings.

Women receive a marriage dowry from their future husbands for their own personal use. Women do not take their husband's name when they marry.

Islamic dress code

Both men and women are expected to dress in a way that is modest and dignified. The following four principles govern Islamic dress code.

ISLAMIC DRESS MUST COVER THE BODY ADEQUATELY

Under Sharia law, for men, the middle part of the body from navel to knee must be covered. And for women, the entire body except hands and face must be covered with material that is not see-through or tight fitting.

ISLAMIC DRESS SHOULD PROVIDE ADORNMENT

Islamic dress should provide a decent appearance, rather than be an eyesore.

ISLAMIC DRESS SHOULD ESTABLISH ISLAMIC IDENTITY

Islamic dress should positively identify people as Muslims.

ISLAMIC DRESS MUST AVOID THREE DEADLY SINS

Islamic dress must be free from showing off, arrogance, and self-indulgence.

Husbands

Muhammad once said: "The most perfect in faith amongst believers is he who is best in manner and kindest to his wife."

The Quran allows men to have four wives.

Inheritance rights of women

Islam was revolutionary in regards to inheritance by women. Prior to the Quranic injunction, women not only did not inherit from their relatives, women themselves were bequeathed as if they were property to be distributed at the death of a husband, father, or brother.

Thus, Islam, by giving women the right to inherit, changed the status of women in an unprecedented fashion.

The Quran states: "Men shall have a share in what parents and kinsfolk leave behind, and women shall have a share in what parents and kinsfolk leave behind." *Quran 4:7.*

In terms of the right to inherit, women and men are equal legal entities.

GLOSSARY OF ISLAMIC TERMS (1)

Allah

Arabic word for "God."

Fatwa

A *fatwa* is an official statement from a Muslim religious leader. *Fatwas* can call for the death of heretics.

Five Pillars

This refers to the Five Pillars of faith (also known as Five Pillars of Islam), which encompass the five fundamental beliefs and actions which are required of all Muslims.

They are: *shahadah, salat, zakat, sawm,* and *hajj.*

Hadith

Hadith are Islamic traditions based on Muhammad's words and deeds that serve as one of the sources of Islamic law.

Hajj

This can refer to any pilgrimage, but normally means the pilgrimage that every Muslim should make to Mecca at least once in his or her life.

Hijra

Literally, this means "to migrate, to sever relations, to leave one's tribe." Throughout the Muslim world, *hijra* refers to the migration of the Prophet Muhammad and his followers to Medina. The year of Muhammad's *hijra* marks the beginning of the Islamic calendar.

Islam

The Arabic term islam means "submission" and itself comes from a word meaning "to surrender," or, "to resign oneself." The word is used as the name of the religion created by Muhammad

between AD 610 and 635. Muhammad himself instituted the name:

"Today I have perfected your religion for you, and I have completed My blessing upon you, and I have approved Islam for your religion."
Quran 5:5

Jihad

The word literally this means "striving" or "struggle," and is used specifically to refer to any struggle against anything or anyone who threatens the Islamic faith. This struggle can occur internally, against temptation and doubt, or externally, against enemies of Islam.

Jihad often refers to "holy war" against non-Muslims.

GLOSSARY OF ISLAMIC TERMS (2)

Mecca

Mecca is a city in the west-central Hejaz area of the Arabian peninsula, where Muhammad was born and began his ministry.

Mullah

This term refers to a member of the Islamic clergy. Usually it refers to a preacher or other low-ranking cleric who has not earned the right to interpret religious laws.

Muhammad

Muhammad was born in AD 570 in Mecca. The name Muhammad means "the Praised one" or "he who is glorified."

Muhammad has another two hundred names, each of which praises some important aspect of his character, such as "Beloved of God," and "Key of Mercy."

Muslim

Literally this means "one who has submitted," and refers to a believer who has submitted to the will of Allah.

Quran

Literally this means "recitation," but specifically refers to the Islamic holy scriptures, which Muhammad received from God through the angel Gabriel. Muhammad had the revelations written down, and they later became the Muslim holy book.

Ramadan

This is the name for the ninth month in the Muslim calendar. During this month, Muslims fast from sunrise to sunset.

S.A.W

This is an acronym which stands for *Sallal-lahu 'alayhi wa-alihi wa-sallam* which means, "Blessings and peace of God be with him and his household."

Muslim writers place this prayer, or the letters "s.a.w" after Muhammad's name whenever it is written.

Sharia

This refers generally to Islamic Law, but in particular the law derived from the Quran, the Sunna of the Prophet, and the consensus of the Muslim community.

Shia

This literally means "party" or "partisans" but refers specifically to the "party of 'Ali and his descendents."

The Shia supported the claims of 'Ali and his line to the right to the leadership of the Muslim community. On this issue they separated from the Sunni in the major schism within Islam.

Sunni

This is the name for the larger of the two major divisions of Islam. The Sunni, who rejected the claims of 'Ali's line, believe that they are the true followers of the *sunna*, the guide to Muslim behavior set out in Muhammad's actions and words

JIHAD

Defining *jihad*

Jihad is holy war. For Muslims, *jihad* is the physical and spiritual struggle against evil. Islam started spreading largely by military conquest. Today most Muslims speak of *jihad* in spiritual terms.

Variety of meanings

The Islamic idea of *jihad* comes from the Arabic root meaning "to strive" or "to make an effort."

Jihad has a wide variety of meanings and interpretations. It can mean an inward spiritual struggle to attain perfect faith.

However, it can also mean an outward material struggle to promote justice and the Islamic social system.

For some Muslims *jihad* is considered the sixth religious duty associated with the five Pillars. This duty requires men to go to war to defend or spread Islam. If they are killed, they are guaranteed eternal life in Paradise.

9/11 and Muslims

The vast majority of Muslims are just as horrified as everyone else by all acts of terrorism and believe that Islam, a religion of mercy, does not allow terrorism or suicide bombers.

Persecution of Christians

The violent interpretation of *jihad* as physical warfare against infidels is encouraged where people live in a culture of poverty and have little hope.